WITH
Lir
FOR DOGS

Graham Chambers Lidiard

WITHDRAWN FROM STOCK

Line Training

FOR DOGS

How it's done

By Monika Gutmann

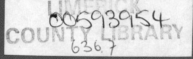
LIMERICK
COUNTY LIBRARY
00593954
636.7

CADMOS

For Dino and Hudson

Copyright of original edition © 2008 Cadmos Verlag GmbH, Im Dorfe 11, 22956 Brunsbek, Germany

Copyright of this edition © 2009 Cadmos Books, Great Britain

Translation: Alexandra Cox

Cover design and layout: Ravenstein + Partner, Verden

Cover all other photos (unless indicated): JBTierfoto

Editorial: Dorothee Dahl and Christopher Long

Printed by: Westermann Druck, Zwickau

All rights reserved: No part of this book may be reprinted or reproduced or utilized
in any form or by any electronic, mechanical, or other means, now known or
hereafter invented, including photocopying and recording, or in any information
storage or retrieval system, without permission in writing from the publisher.

British Library Cataloguing in Publication Data

A catalogue record of this book is available from the British Library.

Printed in Germany

ISBN 978-3-86127-961-7

www.cadmos.co.uk

Contents

Contents

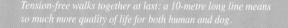

Tension-free walks together at last: a 10-metre long line means so much more quality of life for both human and dog.

Introduction

Do you have a dog that won't come back to you unless he's on a lead or simply does as he pleases when he's off the lead, completely ignoring you out of doors and reckoning that everything else is much more exciting than his human?

Dogs like these commonly spend their lives either on a two-metre lead that's much too short or on an extending lead, unable to enjoy the privilege of running free in meadows and fields because they haven't learned to take notice of their humans and come back on call or whistle. The advice that's often given to anyone owning a dog like this is to give long-line training a try. Many dog-owners, though, fail in the first week. Not many people can explain to them how long-line training works. Just hooking a 10-metre lead to the dog is not the answer. The frustration increases if handling the long lead is tricky: you keep getting tangled up or get terrible friction blisters on your hands or legs, or land on your bottom for the hundredth time. Exasperated, you finally give up and discard the long line and stop letting the dog run free altogether, except in the garden.

What is long-line training?

With well-structured and carefully thought-through long-line training, patience and single-mindedness, you can re-create a happy bond between you and your dog. Your dog will pay better attention to you, will be responsive again and, most important of all, will be sure to come back when called.

Just 10 metres away from success

Long-line training is a safe way to get a dog to learn almost without mistakes. The emphasis here is on 'a way'. There are many ways to work with a dog – it is not our intention here to propagate the one and only true 'training method'. However, because it makes stress-free walks possible, the 10-metre lead brings added quality of life for many dogs and their humans. Long-line training enhances a human's ability to keep a close eye on his or her dog.

This type of training, though, is not for people who expect to see a dog problem that has crept its way in and taken hold over years 'magicked away' after two weeks. Learning is a continuous process – and even things that are unpleasant for the owner are going to get learned. The do-it-yourself approach you've used so far means that your dog has learned that it's more worth his while to keep his nose stuck in the mouse-hole than to listen for your call. In this book, training is always described in terms of positive reinforcement, because this is the most effective and enduring technique for changing and shaping behaviour. You will read more about learning behaviour in dogs in the chapter, 'The most important thing first: how do dogs learn?'.

For people, it is a matter of course to learn everyday things, such as eating with a knife and fork, right from when we're small. Many years of daily repetition enable us to hone this ability. It wouldn't occur to anyone to beat this self-evident social skill into an inquisitive toddler – it is practised and refined day by day by playing. The magic word is learning by succeeding. Whatever is learned needs to be repeated many times and improved so that our 'muscle memory' works properly – and commonly, it won't work the way we'd like it to if we lack the talent, the genetic predisposition or the motivation. You may be asking yourself what genetic predispositions have to do with learning. Well, they have lots to do with it! If we were all the same, we would all have the same abilities.

There'd be no children with learning difficulties, for example, there'd be nobody who wasn't exactly as good at playing chess as at sprinting 100 metres, and we'd all have nothing to fear from hereditary diseases. Unfortunately, our genes dictate otherwise; some people, for example, have 'slow' muscles and no matter how much effort they put into training, they will never be good sprinters. However, if these people were to give long-distance running a try, they would be the successful ones. No two people are alike – and that applies to your dog, too. There are dogs that learn quickly, while others need time and some appear never to make any progress at all.

You cannot expect something from your dog that you have not taught him and that does not suit his natural abilities. A herding dog, for example, will ponder before deciding that a given auditory signal makes sense. True to his breed, he'll come trotting up to you. A border collie, by contrast, will spin round on his hind legs and come hurtling up to you. It is essential to remember these things when you're training your dog.

In my view, a behaviour has been 'learned' when a dog performs an action while I'm standing in front of him in the unlikeliest poses. The world could be coming to an end around him, but I expect a sit from him and he obeys.

This book enables you to follow a step-by-step training plan that provides you with important information about the basic laws of learning and a short introduction to clicker training.

So off we go! Train – don't complain!

In itself, a bell has no meaning for a dog. However, if you ring a bell often enough while feeding the dog, the ringing will trigger a reflex: the dog starts slobbering as soon as he hears the bell.

The most important thing first: how do dogs learn?

We need to spend a little time tackling the theory before we can start with meaningful training. It's like getting your driver's licence: in addition to practical skills, you also need to learn the road traffic rules. The thing to remember in the process is that the basic laws of learning are the same for all vertebrates with brains.

Classical conditioning: the bell rings, the dog salivates

Let's start with classical conditioning. Russian doctor Ivan P. Pavlov discovered this by accident: he noticed that the sight of food alone triggers the flow of saliva (reflex).

If the trigger of the reflex (flow of saliva) is combined with another stimulus – bell-ringing, in this case – the stimulus alone will trigger the salivation, if it is repeated often enough. The dog salivates when the bell rings, even though there's no food nearby.

In simple terms, this means that a stimulus that was neutral before receives another meaning – but no new behaviour is learned. We're all familiar with this from everyday situations: anyone who has had unpleasant experiences at the dentist's only needs to hear the sound of a dental drill to start trembling and getting goosebumps. Anyone who works on a computer a lot knows that a certain acoustic signal announces a new e-mail. There are so many things that we learn unconsciously and associate with feelings without being able to do anything about it. This is precisely the problem with classical conditioning: we do not have it under our control, so it's hard to change it. One example of classical conditioning in dogs is quite simply the doorbell. We never consciously taught our dogs that they have to bark when the doorbell rings, and definitely not that they're supposed to race to the door when they hear it. At first, when the dog hasn't yet learned what happens after the bell, he may just come to the door with you (and this is where he learns that you go to the door after the noise). Once at the door, you attempt to gain some sort of dominance over him. Many visitors also think it's cute when a puppy scampers up to them. So, for the dog this means: ringing = fun at the door is on the cards. With enough repetition – barking is added as the situation develops – we have unconsciously taught the dog that ringing = barking.

It works exactly the same way with the lead that we take off the hook when we're about to go for a walk and the dog starts jumping about. You're sure to know many more examples for your dog.

Summary: classical conditioning
- With classical conditioning a stimulus is learned – not a behaviour!
- Classical conditioning always happens passively, it's not conscious learning.
- Classical conditioning can be controlled with difficulty, if at all.

Operant conditioning: dogs that can run backwards

So, no new behaviour is learned with classical conditioning. Then how come dogs can do tricks – even run backwards – or simply learn how to walk on a lead? This can be explained by operant conditioning. Operant conditioning involves learning by trial and error. It has no recognisable direct triggers, but it does bring about a reaction in the environment. There's a phrase that you should note here: behaviour is determined by its consequence. We've been talking about behaviour all this time: so, what is it? Roughly speaking, behaviour is everything that we do. Sitting, lying, standing and walking are forms of behaviour. Our dogs can do this, too, of course, and lots more – but they only have control over forms of behaviour that belong to their natural behaviour repertoire and are physically possible. These were the findings of Burrhus Frederic Skinner, who performed research on pigeons, rats and other animals back in the 1920s. He coined the term 'operant conditioning'.

So, what happens with operant conditioning? If you want to teach a dog a new behaviour on command, you have two options: reinforcement or punishment. Reinforcements are things (stimuli) that increase the frequency of the shown behaviour after the behaviour: the dog sits down and gets a treat. Correspondingly, punishment is the opposite: the dog barks and gets a clip on the nose. There are two types of reinforcements and two types of punishment: positive and

negative; but please view the terms 'positive' and 'negative' in the mathematical sense: positive = add something, negative = take something away. They're not meant to be regarded as 'good' and 'bad'.

Positive reinforcement means that something pleasant is added after the behaviour. The frequency of the behaviour rises if there is a positive consequence. If the dog comes to me and gets a treat or strokes, he'll come to me more often.

Negative reinforcement means that something unpleasant is removed in the process. For example, there are people who teach a dog how to sit using strangulation by lead. They tug on the lead that's attached to the collar until the dog

Positive working means fun, relaxation and trust for dog and human alike. The brain learns most effectively when relaxed and happy.

sits down. The lead is slackened immediately – being able to breathe is reward enough for the dog. This is a method that is neither dog-friendly nor useful: negative reinforcement encourages avoidance learning. Learning is no fun this way. It makes working with the dog off the lead virtually impossible.

With positive punishment, again, something is added – something unpleasant. If my dog barks, I can interrupt him by giving him a clip on the muzzle. I have added something unpleasant.

Negative punishment is punishment by removing pleasant things: what can I take away from my dog that's pleasant for him? His ball, my company, social contact. If my dog jumps about around me, I turn away and wait until he behaves properly. Once he's got all four paws on the ground, he'll get his strokes. With this example, I have also explained to you how operant learning works: one form of behaviour gets the dog nowhere because he's getting no feedback from the human. However, once he's got all four paws on the ground he gets what he's been after (positive reinforcement) – my affection.

What are reinforcements? There are two types: primary and secondary. Primary reinforcements satisfy biological needs: food or social contact, for example. Secondary reinforcements come about through combining them (by means of classical conditioning, for example) with primary reinforcements – the 'click' in clicker training (see chapter, 'Clicker training') = food for the dog. Money is a secondary reinforcement for us humans. Secondary reinforcements can be put to use considerably more easily and accurately than primary reinforcements.

Our training method in this book will be based only on positive reinforcement and negative punishment/ignoring.

Swiftness is the name of the game

Now, if you want to reward your dog for good work – when practising the 'sit', for example – you need to be pretty quick for one thing, and for another thing the reward needs to be right for the dog.

Quick means really quick: 0.5 seconds is the ideal time, so that the dog can associate the food with what he's done. This is why working with a secondary reinforcement (the clicker, for example) makes communication between human and dog so much easier. I've explained the topic of rewarding specifically in the chapter, 'Rewards – your dog's wages'.

So, for you this means that you need to feed the treat, throw the ball or lavish the praise extremely swiftly. Five seconds later, once your dog has stood up again, praise for the sitting will get you nowhere: this way you're praising your dog for standing up and not for sitting. People often give their dogs the treat very late. When I ask why the dog has received something for standing around, I often hear replies like this one: 'But Fido waited so lovely and patiently just now. That's what it was for.' If I don't know why the dog has received the treat and I'm the trainer/observer, how is the dog supposed to know?

Dogs learn in a specific context and are bad at generalising

When getting in touch with me for the first time, puppy owners very often tell me about all the things their dog can already do: 'He can already sit perfectly, he also comes and lie down is no problem at all. The only thing I want, really, is for my dog to play with other dogs.' However, the reality then proves to be something else. Superpuppy turns out to be average and isn't quite able to strike the required pose in all places. Whose fault is this? Certainly not the stubborn dog's or the disobedient puppy's.

Dogs learn in a specific context. Whatever they're able to do in the living room, they won't be able to do it outside against different backgrounds and with different levels of distraction. The conclusion for you is this: train at all times of day and night, in all locations, against all backgrounds, with many different levels of distraction. The easiest thing to do is to start with not much distraction, increasing it continuously. You will find out how to do this in the chapter 'Building up a command, using the "sit" as an example'.

Act variably

To make sure that a behaviour really takes hold, you need to start rewarding the dog unpredictably. Imagine that, to your dog, you're a bit like a one-armed bandit at the casino. You never know when and how much you're going to win, or whether you mightn't even be able crack the jackpot. If your dog has learned to do some-

thing – sit, for example – and so far you've always rewarded him with a treat, then start only affirming every other sit with a treat. Ultimately, your dog mustn't know whether he's going to be rewarded or what he's going to get. In matters of rewarding you need to be unpredictable to your pet and, as such, ever fascinating. You will find out how to put rewards to use in the chapter, 'Rewards – your dog's wages'.

> **Summary: operant conditioning**
> ◆ Operant conditioning is learning by trial and error.
> ◆ Behaviour is determined by its consequence.
> ◆ Behaviour that has a positive consequence is shown more frequently.
> ◆ Dogs learn in a specific context.
> ◆ Dogs are bad at generalising.
> ◆ Reinforce every desired behaviour at first.
> ◆ Reinforce variably later on.

Thoughts about punishment

If we take a look at punishment among dogs, this form of upbringing only finds application in the social environment: for example, when a mother dog nips her puppies after multiple warnings when personal space or resources are at stake. A dog that is bitten by a snake is 'punished' for his brazenness – in future, he'll know that certain animals have a tendency towards aggression: learning for life, in order to survive. However, dogs do not teach themselves to sit or come back on command.

Therefore, in my view, there is no justification for handling a dog aggressively or by inflicting pain for the purpose of learning, consolidating or triggering a behaviour that is required for cohabitation with humans.

With 'positive' punishment, I do something unpleasant to my dog – a jerk on the lead, for example.

I'd like to spend a few more explanatory words on the above method of punishment, so that you'll understand why we say no to it.

1. Punishment needs to take place at the first attempt. For you this means, exactly as is the case with rewarding, that you must punish your dog for misbehaviour straight away. If you do not do this, your dog will not recognise what he's being punished for. Once he has got away with whatever he's doing, he'll quickly learn to tell when a punishment is to be expected and when it's not. As the person giving out the punishment, you're usually around; your dog will learn that the undesired deed (lying on the couch, for example) is not allowed in your presence. If, on the other hand, you're not around, your dog is allowed to jump on to the couch with impunity again. The punishment therefore made no sense.

2. Punishment must achieve maximum intensity straight away. Are you able to punish your dog a) immediately and b) so harshly that he'll never do something again? People have been known to start off with 'gentle' punishments, which the dog quickly gets used to. The dog is then accused of naughtiness or having a thick skull because he continues to do forbidden things. The punishment is doled out in gradually increasing doses, but the behaviour doesn't change. The spiral of violence continues, and the dog is written off as untrainable. Maybe the dog ends up biting because he doesn't understand the point of the training. If you need to punish a misbehaviour more than twice, your dog will not perceive the punishment as being a punishment.

3. Punishment must always take place for the same misbehaviour. You must therefore be able to guarantee 100 per cent that you are able to punish the same situation at all times. Can you guarantee that? If you paid attention to point 2, you only needed to punish once or twice at the very most anyway.

4. Punishment needs to be recognisable to the dog as punishment. Physical beating is not really perceived as a punishment by many dogs. Punishment is meant to bring about an unpleasant internal status, so that next time the dog will avoid the situation or the unwanted behaviour. Whether you're inflicting it on your dog physically or using a water pistol, rattler or similar, you need to know whether the dog actually experiences it as a punishment. Many dogs end up getting used to a punishment like this, so the point of this method would also be awry. I know plenty of dogs whose owners tried to discourage them from doing something by using a spray collar. Unfortunately it was in vain, because these dogs didn't mind the squirting at all. In these cases, a lot of money was spent for a useless object. The money would probably have been more usefully invested in a good dog training school.

5. Punishment breaks up actions, but it does not generate new forms of behaviour. It only teaches your dog to avoid certain situations.

It's up to you to decide, though, what he's meant to do instead.

6. Punishment should take place anonymously. This becomes problematic, as well, if we consider points 1 and 2. You would need to think up and install devices even before your dog committed a misdeed so that he couldn't get to the table or worktop to take food in the first place. This way you would be able to make sure that he didn't associate the punishment with you, and you would be able to give out the punishment the first time. However, whether the anonymous punishment was harsh enough to have a lasting impact on your dog is a question that remains open.

Punishment has an effect on the person giving out the punishment, though: they get all worked up in the punishing, not noticing that they are 'classically conditioning' themselves in the process and are themselves unable to do otherwise. The person doing the punishing loses sight of the things that need rewarding, and the object of the punishment becomes incapable of responding to positive attention. You see how difficult it is to punish properly. This is why you should refrain from any application of violence towards your dog (even a jerk on the lead is an application of violence). Give some thought to what your dog is actually allowed to do. Instead of taking on the risk of misjudged positive punishment as a result of poor timing and application, reward your dog for the things he does right.

No dog that I know of so far has been harmed by a misjudged treat, but by a misjudged punishment – yes.

An example:
punishment is difficult to control.

We were out on a stud farm with a puppy-training class. A small millstream runs through it and a goat field, sealed off with an electric fence, extends along the stream. We give out repeated warnings not to let the puppies get to the fences so that this negative experience can be avoided.

As a result of inattentiveness, a puppy came into direct contact with the goat fence by the millstream. The young dog cried out terrifyingly and was really distressed. What do you think the dog associated with the electric shock? The wire? No – he saw the stream at the moment of the 'punishment'. Another time when we were back at the stud farm, the puppy would not go near the millstream. We had to feed enormous quantities of tasty treats to the timorous dog to get him to approach the 'bad' stream little by little and put his paws in the water.

See how difficult it is to control and apply punishment precisely and effectively, so that the punished dog doesn't associate it with everything except the 'misdemeanour' that you intended?

Therefore, keep away from pointless application of violence – it does more harm than good.

Here, the Labrador gets a reward for a correctly performed sit.

Rewards –
your dog's wages

There are people who believe that dogs only need to carry out 'orders' out of fondness or even gratitude. In their view, this should be enough. I find this idea highly presumptuous. Dogs, just like humans, seek their success and advantage in what they do.

So, how is the term 'reward' defined in general? 'Reward: a return or recompense for service or merit.'

(Oxford English Dictionary)

'A reward is a major motivation in encouraging readiness to perform.'

(Wikipedia, 2007)

Why reward?

Through rewards, the dog learns that there is an advantage for him in being near his human. Why should a dog come back to you when, after all, he's having much more fun doing what he's doing right now (digging in the mouse hole)? If you're boring and irritable and, what's more, sending out these signals to your dog from 100 metres away, what's going to persuade your dog to run to a killjoy in a bad mood? Think this is exaggerated? Not at all! I know plenty of dogs that ignore their owners out of doors and simply stop taking notice of them. This is precisely because these owners are bipeds who, a bit like lighthouses, constantly indicate their position and current mood by calling and who are lost in their own thoughts.

It is not a matter of course that your dog should feel a bond with you, just because you treat him to a walk three times a day and serve him food every morning and night. Bonding with the dog is something the human needs to work on, not the dog! After all, we regard ourselves to be the cleverer animal of the two. Accordingly, our dog should be entitled to expect us to empathise with his world, not the other way round.

Change your attitude and make it clear to your dog that something good is to be had from you, that it's possible to ignore mouse holes and that the human out of doors can be every bit as interesting as the human at home. It won't hurt you to pay your dog for things he does well. After all, you work for money– or is your boss such a nice guy that you gladly let him have your wages?

The dog sits expectantly in front of his dog trainer. The person is not holding a treat.

The dog trainer now reaches into the pouch of treats to fetch the reward. The dog is required to wait in the desired position throughout.

The dog receives the treat whilst remaining in the sitting position.

The situation is ended on a clear command.

View the rewards as a 'pay cheque' for your dog, so that he comes reliably even when it appears that there's something more interesting somewhere else – and even when you have no treats on you. You will find more about how dogs learn in the chapter, 'The most important thing first: how do dogs learn?'.

What is the difference between rewarding and enticing?

With rewarding, the person does not hold the treat during the exercise. However, since you always need to be very quick with the rewards when building up a new exercise, a secondary reinforcement (clicker) is a big help during the process (see chapter, 'The most important thing first: how do dogs learn?').

This way, your dog really learns to do things consciously on command. It also means that you needn't panic about the dog not doing something when you haven't got any treats on you; the dog has learned to wait for more commands from you even if there are no treats immediately to hand. There'll be something to make up for that later. When enticing your dog, you hold the treat and the dog merely follows the hidden scent.

Imagine that you need to find the post office in a town you don't know. Somebody holds a £50 note in front of your nose and uses this method to lead you to the nearest post office. Have you taken any notice of the surroundings and taken an exact note of the route? No. You didn't need to, either, because you had somebody with you to lead the way. If you need to get the post office on your own now, you'll probably find it quite difficult.

This is enticing: the dog merely runs after the treat without being consciously aware of his posture.

Enticing is only permissible in a limited number of training structures, perhaps to trigger a particular kind of behaviour that the dog wouldn't show straight away of his own volition. The reward has to be given immediately afterwards though, if you're not working with the clicker.

When's the time to reward?

Reward your dog for things that he does right. If he comes up to you voluntarily during a walk, give him a reward to let him know that it's worth his while to pop by and see you, as recognition of a praiseworthy deed. After all, it is not a matter of course that your dog should maintain feedback and contact, and keep a constant eye on where you're going. If it was, you wouldn't be reading this book. The most precise way to declare to your dog what he's done right is to work with a secondary reinforcement (see chapter, 'Clicker training').

What's the reward?

Verbal praise and a pat on the head have got to be enough, you say? Poor dog! Dogs commonly don't notice that verbal praise is meant to be a reward; also, rewarding really needs to be viewed by the dog as being 'wages for a counter-performance'. Most people, moreover, give verbal praise in the same vocal pitch that they use for telling off. How is the dog supposed to tell when the mumbled 'Good boy' is intended to be praise, when 'Bad boy' in the same tone is meant to be a telling-off?

To convince the dog initially that running up a ladder is worth his while, you can entice him. The enticing morsels are discontinued later.

A pat on the head is not necessarily a suitable reward. Little Nero here is showing that he's uneasy: his ears are laid back flat, his eyes closed and he has turned his back on the person.

0059139754
LIMERICK
COUNTY LIBRARY

Nero is visibly more comfortable this way. The person is on a level with him and is stroking him gently on his back and side.

Dogs do not understand the content of our words, they interpret our tone of voice and our posture. If you bend over the dog, patting his head in the process what's more, this is anything but praise.

Just watch how often your dog takes a step back from you when you come up to him with this kind of reward.

What can people use to reward dogs?

These can be really tasty treats. Make a little effort and test various snacks on your dog, keeping a list of the favourites at the same time:

Treats – favourites for Fido:
1. Sausages
2. Gouda
3. Apple
4. Banana
5. Chicken
6. _____

Proceed in exactly the same way with things from the social side:

Actions – favourites for Fido:
1. Swimming
2. Throwing balls
3. Racing against me
4. Sniffing
5 Digging in mouse hole
6. _____

How do you find out what's on the list of favourite treats? Prepare a few different rewarding snacks, such as sausages, various varieties of cheese, fruit, vegetables and dog treats from the pet-food shop.

Test 1: Sausage/Gouda
Test 2: Sausage/apple
Test 3: Apple/banana
Test 4: Turkey breast/sausage

Pick up a piece of each variety, one in your left hand, one in your right. Show your dog the treats with your palms open. The treat your dog eats first will usually be the priority. To make sure of this, repeat the test with the chosen treats a few more times. If you can recognise a clear trend, write it down. Try out various combinations and this way you'll be able to compile the list of favourites.

You have now given some thought as to what your dog enjoys; you have really shown an interest and paid him some attention. This is the first step towards a real bond. Now you have a broad range of treats to reward your dog. In addition, you should always take care to suit the treats to the task. If your dog needs to master a difficult task, feel free to make it something especially good – and you're also allowed to increase the amount. If your dog has managed to climb a ladder unassisted the first

time around, give him a whole handful of treats! Show him that he's done well, and pay him for it. Does your dog love swimming? Make use of that by training next to a lake or river, for example, and then send him off swimming as an extra-big reward! Try to find out what your dog will recognise as a reward at that specific moment. This is truly a step towards a harmonious life together.

Summary: rewarding correctly

- List what your dog really enjoys eating and make a list of favourites.
- List what your dog really enjoys doing and make a list of favourites.
- Alternate between food and play when rewarding.
- Vary the amount of food or the length of time playing when rewarding.

Although the dog isn't paying any attention at all, the owner is trying to get the dog to sit. He's attempting to do this – as is often the case, unfortunately – by pressing down on the rear end and tugging on the lead. However, this is not the way to teach the dog to pay attention to you and your commands, even when the situation is tense.

Building up a command,
using the 'sit' as an example

Before we continue with the training, I would like to explain to you – using the auditory and visual 'sit' command as an example – how to build up a command meaningfully. You will find out how basic learning works in dogs and all other vertebrates in the chapter, 'The most important thing first: how do dogs learn?'. You can use the method used here for building up the 'sit' command for any chosen command that you'd like to teach your dog.

Your dog is totally indifferent to what you say to him to make him perform an action. He does not understand the meaning of the word: you could equally teach him to sit down by using the auditory signal 'washing machine'. It is important, though, that you do teach him to do it. If we examine the auditory signal 'Sit', the dog is required to perform the following action: he places his backside on the ground. For the dog, the word 'sit' is simply a sound! When saying it, you also need to pay attention to your voice, body language and posture. More often than not, the person stands leaning forward – therefore extremely threateningly – in front of the dog, dangles a treat or, even worse, tugs on lead and collar and presses down on the dog's bottom.

What's more, the person repeats the funny sound 'Sitsitsitsit' in many different tones. Or says things like, 'Sit nicely now! Good boy sit! A nice sittly-wittly!' until in the end the person loses patience, snaps at the dog, 'Sit, I said!' and the dog sits down out of surprise or fear. Remember: the meaning of the word is totally alien to the dog! He can hear his human making some sort of sounds, feels threatened by the posture, and in the end he is 'growled at' and reprimanded for something that he can't do and doesn't know. This isn't exactly encouraging for a trusting relationship or fun while learning. You therefore need to teach your dog clearly and in a friendly way what meaning the sound 'Sit' is supposed to have for him. This is just like the way in which you would need to learn a foreign language: word for word, and taking cues from various inflections, as well.

'Sit' is a simple command. A dog can learn quickly how to perform it.

Learning cues

The new cue that the dog is going to learn is 'Sit'. This means that the dog associates the sound 'Sit' with the action 'place bottom on the ground'. As far as possible, he is to do it at all times of day and night, against all likely and unlikely backgrounds, preferably at all possible distances, with all forms of posture from the person, in every conceivable tone of voice and at all levels of distraction. This apparently simple cue is clearly quite formidable!

What do you need to remember?
- The cue should be as simple as possible, such as 'Sit'.
- Always say the cue in the same friendly and high-pitched tone.
- Use a visual signal to go with it, such as a raised index finger.

Let your dog have a quick sniff so that he knows that you have something tasty in your hand. While doing so, stand or crouch upright in front of the dog and raise your hand slightly to the rear above the dog's head so that he is obliged to follow the hand with his eyes.

Please never forget that the cue is 'Sit' and not 'Sitsitsitsitsit!'. To the dog, these are two completely different cues.

Start the exercise at a location where there's not much distraction. Put a particularly tasty treat in your right hand; the index finger is raised, the treat concealed beneath the closed remaining fingers.

Let your dog take a quick sniff so that he knows that there's something good in your hand. Stand upright in front of your dog, now raise your right hand slightly to the rear above the dog's head so that he is obliged to follow the hand with his eyes.

In order to continue following the hand with his eyes, your dog is now forced to sit down. While your dog is now placing his bottom on the ground, say the new word, 'Sit'. Now give your dog the treat from your right hand straight away. Important! Give him the treat while he still has his bottom on the ground.

Please do not give the dog the treat once he's stood up again. If you do, you will have to repeat the exercise. Otherwise, you will be teaching him that the command 'sit' means 'place bottom on the ground – stand up'. You'll then be wondering why your dog is incapable of sitting for longer periods.

Right from the very beginning, try to stand upright in front of your dog and hold your hand slightly behind the dog's head.

Raised index finger, initially pointing behind/over the dog's head.

While the dog is moving (placing bottom on the ground) say the cue once:' Sit' and always in the same tone!

Repeat the exercise four or five times with the treat in your hand. The sequence is always the same.

Then you start doing the exercise without the treat in your right hand, this time keeping the treat concealed in your left hand so that

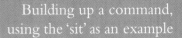

Feed dog immediately he has his bottom on the ground.

Only feed the dog in the 'bottom on ground' position.

you can reward more swiftly. The sequence of this exercise differs slightly from the exercise with the treat.

- Raised index finger.
- You say 'Sit' and wait until your dog places his bottom on the ground.

Repeat this variation four to five times as well before also discontinuing with the treat in your left hand. Instead, get the treat out of a pouch or out of a small bowl placed within easy reach. Again, please take care to feed the dog in the right position.

Ultimately, you retrieve the treat from a bowl or pouch. The dog remains in his position throughout.

Potential problems and solutions to these problems

Problem: Your dog keeps hopping about around you.

Solution: Wait calmly until your dog has quietened down. Let him hop and jump, do not talk to him while he is doing so, do not tell him off – just wait. He will learn that hopping about will not get him to his treat.

Problem: The dog keeps gnawing and licking your hand holding the treat.

Solution: Raise your hand so that he can't get to it. Do not feed until the dog behaves quietly and keeps his bottom on the ground.

Problem: Your dog stands up again straight away.

Solution: Always feed the dog in the desired position. You need to be very quick at first. Never feed the dog if he is not in the desired position.

Problem: Your dog does not sit down, but shifts backwards.

Solution: Check your body language. Dogs often feel threatened when you lean over them. Start the exercise crouching or kneeling.

Problem: Your dog does not sit down after the verbal command 'Sit'.

Solution: When giving your command, count slowly up to 15. If your dog does not sit, change position with your dog, move two steps sideways. There, give the 'sit' command again. Pay attention to your tone of voice. Have you really been saying the word 'sit' in the same friendly way every time?

Why are you meant always to reward your dog in the right position? The dog associates the reward with the position that he's in – so if he stands up, you've rewarded him for standing, not for the actual 'sit' exercise.

Why do we not simply press down on the dog's bottom? Dogs learn in a specific context (see the chapter, 'The most important thing first: how do dogs learn?'), so that means that the dog connects the cue 'sit' with the tactile signal 'pressing on bottom' and the verbal signal. I know a number of dogs that are therefore incapable of sitting down on the 'sit' command at a distance because the contact is not there.

Consolidating the exercise

You have now taught your dog the cue 'sit' in the kitchen. However, that doesn't mean that your dog will realise that 'sit' has the same meaning in the living-room (bottom on ground). As you know, dogs are very bad at generalising, and it is our responsibility to make sure that our four-legged friend has the chance to learn this new cue in all possible inflections, so to speak. Relocate your exercises from the living-room to the bedroom, the hall, to stony ground, tarmac, grass – you're bound to think of more places. Make sure that the distractions increase gradually. You can't expect a lightning-quick sit from a puppy in the middle of a crowded department store – if he's able to sit down on command at all, that is, with so much distraction around.

The surrounding stimuli there are far too great for him to be able to concentrate on learning

words – have you ever tried teaching the two-times-table to a first-year primary-school child in a toy department?

Important Tips

- Say 'Sit' only once, while the dog is sitting down, in conjunction with the visible signal (raised index finger). Pay attention to your tone of voice when giving the verbal command.
- To start off with, reward from the hand that you use to give the visible signal.
- Reward the dog immediately and in the correct position (bottom on the ground).
- After repeating several times, give the verbal command 'sit' before the dog sits, and always in conjunction with the visible signal.
- Give the reward in the correct position from your left hand or from the pouch.
- Practise in many different places and with increasing levels of distraction. Always reward straight away when there are new requirements.
- Vary the reward sequences – in familiar situations (kitchen, living-room) where your dog sits reliably on command, reward only every other, then every third sit.
- Vary the rewards – with time, caviar every day stops being a motivation. Experiment with the treats. Your dog must never know what's going to pop out for him and his work.

Be consistent! When you say 'Sit', mean it, no matter how hectic things are around you. Nothing is worse than a signal that is not performed. Your dog is not meant to be left wondering what the priority is right now, so if your dog doesn't do on command what you have taught him to do, you have raised the requirements too quickly and your dog is not yet able to do it. Wait a moment until your dog is responsive again, move aside a little and give your command once more. This works in most cases.

If you notice that your dog is so distracted that he's not going to follow the command, then don't give it! Move on and give your command in a quieter spot.

Important! During the training phases, never give the dog a treat when he does something 'wrong' – doesn't sit down for example, runs away or hops about. To the dog the treat means, 'Well done!' So, if you throw a treat at him for simply taking a look around, what does he learn from this? That taking a look around is good. If you have no treat on you, praise in a quiet tone of voice, so that the dog is not tempted to jump up. A treat given five minutes afterwards is the last thing you need, though – your dog won't know what he's getting it for.

To work with the long line, you need a normal or so-called Norwegian harness.

The long line and other accessories for training

Harness

Before you can clip on the long line, you need a well-fitting, padded harness for the dog. When buying, look out for a broad, soft strap and padding that won't get soggy when it rains.

A suitable harness is one with two D-rings for daily use: one at the front on the neck and one over the middle back.

A fitting Norwegian harness is also extremely comfortable for the dog to wear, the advantage being that the dog doesn't need to step through a loop. It is simply pulled over the head and secured in place by means of a belly strap.

You should take care to ensure good fitting and comfort, particularly with short-haired, muscular dogs. The harness mustn't dig in anywhere or injure the dog. So-called 'step-in' harnesses are less advisable.

Important! Never do long-line training with a normal collar, choker chain, studded collar or even a Halti head collar! With boisterous dogs, these can result in injuries to the neck vertebrae and larynx. If you use a head collar (Halti), you can even kill a boisterous dog with it; if he runs into the line, you could break his neck as a result of the sudden halt.

So-called 'step-in' harnesses are less advisable.
A dog with a narrow chest or a particularly clever fellow canine would soon slip out of this harness.

The long line
and other accessories
for training

An advisable line for small dogs and puppies is shown in the middle. The black line in the foreground is for a medium-sized dog, and the belt leashes and the thick red line are suitable for particularly strong dogs.

Long line

Now we come to the other central piece of equipment, the long line. For your own safety, you should not skimp on price here. High-quality lines are durable, weather-resistant and easy-care.

For puppies and small dogs

Lines for puppies and small dogs must be as light as possible. However, light lines often have the disadvantage that they are really thin. Round lines for small dogs and puppies should be three to four millimetres thick.

This is why good, leather-padded cycling or weight-lifting gloves are a 'must' if you own a big puppy, or you could get unpleasant friction burns on your hands. In addition, remember to get a line that does not quickly become saturated with water, so that it doesn't get too heavy. After all, you want your puppy to run and jump. Lines made from modern synthetic material are ideal.

For bigger young dogs and adult dogs

For young dogs and adult dogs, you should always buy a line to match size and weight. A mastiff can shoot off pretty quickly, and a good line should be able to withstand this.

The best thing is a non-slip round line, approximately 10 to 12 millimetres, or a 25-millimetre belt leash that doesn't shed threads or fibres and become saturated. With belt leashes, ensure that they are not woven from cotton, because cotton becomes saturated very quickly and gets very heavy. Sopping-wet lines like these are no fun, especially during the transitional months in spring and autumn. With bigger dogs, also always use cycling or weight-lifting gloves, as well, simply to protect yourself against injuries. A belly strap with panic hook is advisable as a back-up with big dogs. This ensures that your arm is not pulled out of joint when the dog shoots off, or that you are able to let go of the line in an instant without putting yourself in danger.

Panic hook

Why is an extendable lead no good?

Extendable leads are, of course, handy if the dog has not been taught to run nicely on a standard two-metre leash. However, these boxes are an absolute no-no for long-line training. Firstly, these are clunky boxes that can only be held in one hand. Secondly, a number of material defects have been known. Thirdly, small dogs can feel the pull. Fourthly, it is impossible to let go of the end at short notice if the dog has bounded into the bushes somewhere and has got tangled up.

Once, a German shepherd that was being walked on the road on an extendable lead ran in front of my car. He spotted a cat on the other side and ran off. By the time his owner had pressed the stop button and was trying to reel back the dog, he was standing three metres into the road, brought to a halt by the stop. I always drive extra carefully when I see dogs with extendable leads, and this time that saved that German shepherd's life.

With a two-metre lead there would have been only two possibilities:

a) The dog wouldn't have got into the road in the first place, because his owner would have been hanging on behind (provided that she was paying attention).

The long line
and other accessories
for training

Treat pouch

b) The dog would have had a chance to get to the other side of the road without being halted on the road mid-run and getting caught by a car.

Both variants are risky.
However, a two-metre lead comes to an end after two metres, while an extendable lead provides more opportunities for risky behaviour.

To ensure that you have your treat within reach at all times, a separate pouch is advisable. A belt bag isn't quite so recommendable, as the opening is too narrow for the treat to be reached quickly enough. Special treat pouches, which can be secured quickly to belt buckle, trousers or jacket pocket, have proved their worth in practice. They have a wide opening and are also washable.

A variety of practical pouches for treats is now available. They are very handy because you can secure them to your belt or waistband, plus they are washable and extremely durable.

A human steps in as a replacement dog to start off with, so that you can practise winding and unwinding the line without stress.

Preparatory training

Before starting the long-line training, it is imperative to do a few dry runs using the 10-metre line. This will stop you getting tangled up in the line and preserve you from unlovely encounters with fields and forest floors. After all, you are meant to give your full concentration to your dog. To this end, it is very important that you absorb the technique of winding and unwinding thoroughly. Practice makes perfect! Ideally, practise the winding technique with a partner, or have your children play at being dogs! Go for a walk with your training partner and provide sufficient line so that your partner (later dog) has no need to pull. Your dog will have plenty of opportunity to make full use of the line's 10 metres later on.

This is how it should look when you start the training with your dog. The line is wound up loosely in the left hand, while you can use your right hand to grasp the line.

If your partner slows down, wind the line up again. You should really practise this technique of winding and unwinding so that it becomes second nature. This way you'll be able to forget about the line and give your full concentration to your dog.

Pay no attention to your dog when you start with the orientation training.

Orientation training

Orientation training is, for one thing, an extremely good exercise for handling the long line with the dog on the end. For another thing, this exercise, which is necessary for dogs of all ages as an accompaniment to long-line training, will refocus your dog's attention on you. It is based on the dog's free will – you play a rather passive role. If you have a dog that reacts aggressively towards people or fellow dogs, please read the chapter, 'Long-line training with aggression problems' now!

Find open land where there's not much distraction. You have your dog, the 10-metre line and plenty of really good treats. It all hangs on your dog's motivation! The dog is on the long

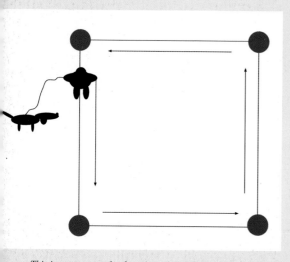

This is your course for the orientation training.

line (don't forget the harness!) and you now walk an imaginary square about 20 metres long.

Your dog runs alongside you, ahead of you, behind you. The most important thing is that you pay no attention to your dog. No matter what he is doing at the moment – you walk your 20-metre route! Paying no attention means that you do not talk to him, you do not look at him, you do not click your tongue or slap your leg.

As soon as your dog comes to you and makes contact: give him a treat! Praise him and then send him away again with a jolly 'Off you go!' and a dismissing hand movement.

If your dog nevertheless continues to hop about around you, simply pay him no attention. He will notice that he'll get nowhere with you by hopping about, and will soon turn his attention to other things. Be firm with yourself and really pay no attention to your dog. No laughing, no looking! Do not scold your dog either if he bites the line, nips your calf or shows any other kind of attention-seeking behaviour. In such situations, keep your nerve, stop and wait until your dog has calmed down. Then continue walking your imaginary 20 by 20-metre square.

Attention-grabbing behaviour (jumping up, biting trousers) must be ignored. Be really firm and do not look at or talk to your dog.

Stand at the corners of the square for a little while. There, count slowly up to 100. If your dog has not come to you within that time, continue walking. If your dog comes up to you while you are counting, affirm his action with a treat and then continue.

Remember to wind and unwind the long line continually throughout the process. This way

Even if your dog finds this unusual at first, do not let him make you lose your calm.

You must affirm all voluntary, attentive contact by your dog with a treat immediately: if he comes to you and looks at you, give him a treat or click and reward.

He stops and looks back at you: praise or click and reward. Your dog doesn't need to make direct eye contact. Dogs have a broader field of vision than humans do and perceive us even when they are not looking us directly in the eye.

the correct routine with the line will become a habit entirely unconsciously, so that even on tricky terrain, you have the knack of the technique as if doing it in your sleep.

Orientation training is fundamental for successful long-line training. This way the dog learns that voluntarily coming back and paying attention to his human brings him success, that is, a treat. Dogs that have a big attention deficit should be fed the daily food ration during orientation training.
Let dogs work for their food!

To start off with, always train in places where there is no distraction for your dog. This is particularly important for puppies, so that they really learn to concentrate on you. The distraction is increased continuously during training – do not proceed too quickly with this.

Training schedule for orientation exercises

You should carry out the orientation training at least twice daily. Time allocation should be staggered according to your dog's age:
* Puppies 8 to 20 weeks, approximately 5 minutes
* Young dogs from approximately 5 months, 10 to 15 minutes
* Dogs from approximately 12 months, 30 to 45 minutes.

Levels of distraction – duration of training

1. Open land without distraction – approximately two weeks
You will most often find open land with no distractions outside your town or village or in isolated corners of parks. If you train in inner-city parks, please ensure that you're less likely to encounter dogs off the lead. In big cities there's always a little piece of open land somewhere that's not busy. When heading off to open land outside, don't forget your poop bag and make sure that the grass is short – you should avoid entering fields where the grass is more than ankle-deep. These are fields for food crops, and farmers do not always react in a friendly manner when one runs across these fields with one's dog.

2. Open land with slight distraction – approximately three weeks
The slight distraction should come from a path some distance away where there are sometimes cyclists and walkers and so on.

3. Open land with moderate distraction – approximately three weeks
Here you should seek out an open space that is located in a park, but not at busy times such as summer weekends when lots of people are looking for a place in the park. You can save this for the last part of the training.

4. Open land with a lot of distraction – approximately three weeks
Now you can go on to open land where there are lots of people and dogs in direct proximity – for example, parks where dogs on leads are allowed. Train in car parks or other busy areas that you know of.

Vary the length of your long line after you have completed the first week of training at one training level. You can tie a knot in the line every metre and thus determine how long the line is. Keep to one length of line per unit of training. Give your dog the chance to work out for himself how much space he can use, and to adapt to this space.

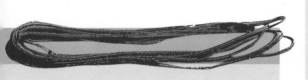

The training duration is approximate and indicated to provide you with a basis. You can start the training at the next level of distraction once your dog is maintaining feedback with you at all times, is attentive even when distracted and does not get annoyed by distraction. One dog, for example, may need longer for distraction level 2 than another dog does. Only make the transition to the next training step once it gets really boring for your dog. If he still reacts to distractions from time to time, you must wait before changing to the next level.

Keep a training diary. Make a note of date, place and length of the training.

What incidents came up? What went particularly well? This way you'll always have an overview of what distractions you still need to practise on. This will ensure that you do not proceed too quickly.

Potential problems and solutions
Problem: Your dog refuses to walk on.
Solution: Your patience is called for here. Wait until your dog stands up again, and really go for it! Praise him, play with him, tumble about with him. End the training after the play. In the summer, please ensure that you train at cool times of the day. Train where the dog has the possibility to go swimming, for example.
Problem: Your dog sees a distraction and tries to get to it.
Solution: Stop and wait until your dog turns round to you. Praise him lavishly and have lots of fun with him (tumble, play, throw treats).
Problem: You have the impression that your dog doesn't come to you often enough.
Solution: Your patience is called for here, as well. Your dog has to discover how to learn independently at some point. There are dogs with extreme attention deficit or that don't realise that they can change things through their own action. At first, these dogs need a really long time before they've grasped that there's something in it for them if they stay close to the human. Once it's clicked though, the next training steps will be easier to master. The only real help in this case is extreme patience and a reward for every little move closer that the dog makes.

This is how the puppy gets to know the long line as something pleasant – walks and games together encourage bonding.

Everyday long-line training

The training can be carried out in a similar way for dogs of all ages. I've dealt with important details specifically in sub-chapters, so that any unclear points can be eliminated as far as possible. It goes without saying that the dog always wears the harness on walks. You should never walk your dog on a long line and collar.

Walks with puppies and young dogs

At first, your puppy follows you like a shadow; after all, it is important to follow one's reference person. For the dog, this guarantees shelter and protection, social contact, safety and food.

So why should you put your puppy on a lead at all during your short walks? Because this way, you have him under control – after all, you always take your small child's hand when the situation is unpredictable. You are simply making your puppy safe with the long line. It means that you will never be in the awkward position of having to run after your four-legged friend because there's danger ahead, for example. Your little bundle of fur needs to learn to come to you in dangerous situations and when

he's afraid, instead of fleeing somewhere in a panic. Imagine that there's a bang and your dog runs out of his wits towards a main road. Not a nice picture.

The additional benefit of the long line with a puppy is that you won't need to get him used to it later on. Not all dogs need to be put on the long line at five to six months old, but when they are older the long line is used very frequently. The box on page 47 explains why this is the case.

At any rate you should make the effort, because what you teach your puppy now will only need to be consolidated and engrained later. Unlearning unpleasant behaviours that have already crept in over months or even years means that even more intensive work is called for, which is why you must not let your puppy make mistakes!

Discarded paper handkerchiefs should preferably be left where they are.

Puppies do not need very long walks at first. Four to five times daily of 10 to 15 minutes is totally sufficient for dogs up to about six months old. Keep in mind that joints and bones are still very soft and pliable. For one thing, you can always combine a small unit of the orientation training with a short walk. For another, you're allowing your puppy to discover the world in a relaxed way. If your puppy has discovered something fantastic, go to him and join him in taking a look at what's there. Discovering the world together encourages bonding.

If your puppy has something in his mouth that doesn't meet with your approval, do a swap. Show him a delicious morsel of food or get out his favourite toy. If he drops what he's got in his mouth in return, say 'Drop' as he's doing so and give him the morsel of food/toy straight away. Pay attention that he doesn't pick up what he's spat out again – place one of your feet on it. Pay attention that you don't throw the exchanged item away – this will draw your dog's attention to it again! If you are holding it, raise it slowly, put it in your pocket for now and dispose of it discreetly later. Then ask him to run with you with a jolly 'Come on!'. As your dog is on the long line, you have a great opportunity to practise this. Your dog cannot run off ahead of you and turn it into a merry chase. Rather, you are able to act calmly and make him a better offer. Your puppy learns to trust you this way, because your attitude is confident and poised. Once your puppy has made the association that he does not need to keep his 'treasures'

Swap his 'treasures' for a similarly good 'treasure'. This way your puppy will learn not to run off ahead of you with booty.

safely away from you, he will start bringing you things. Be glad about this! Your puppy trusts you and you can always decide whether he is allowed to keep something or is going to get something less risky in exchange.

Read the section, 'Building up recall' to find out what you need to practise on walks.

Why many young dogs suddenly stop 'hearing' from the age of about five/six months:

The reasons behind this are quite simply to do with development. Every organism continues to develop; in biology, this is known as ontogenesis. Some behaviours and physical changes only start at certain ages. The most clearly visible example for both humans and dogs is the onset of sexual maturity and the puberty associated with it.

In the young dog, the hunting instinct is awakened at five to six months of age. In the case of original hunting dog breeds, this can happen even earlier. Odours and movements take on a new meaning and the dog follows his genetic predispositions. Birds are frightened off for fun, the neighbour's cat gets chased up the tree and noses get stuck in the nearest mouse-holes.

This is why you should get your puppy used to the long line straight away. Then you will be able to engrain commands that have already been learned during the young dog phase and continue to prevent your dog from making mistakes.

Walks with older dogs

To make sure that the long-line training goes well, your dog must be put on the long line for every walk. If you have been working through this book from the beginning, you will, of course, have plenty of experience with handling the line by now. You will find out what you need to practise on your walks in the following chapters.

Building up recall

You should start recall training straight away, especially with puppies. Please note that your presence must always be something positive for your puppy; he needs to look forward to being with you.

The same thing applies if you have a dog that has so far failed to come or only comes after several calls: again, your dog needs to enjoy being with you. You have prepared the ground for this with the orientation training (see section, 'Orientation training'). You can and should practise recall and orientation in parallel.

Choose a simple and easy-to-remember cue. A friendly 'Here' is suitable for this purpose. If you have already used this cue and your dog fails to come on this command, try something else. For example, a whistle is loud, always sounds the same and can always be heard, even in high wind; onomatopoeic words such as 'Yee-haa' are also suitable. The dog doesn't mind what cue means 'come back'. The only important thing is that you do teach him this cue.

From a tonal point of view, 'ee' sounds are high-pitched and friendly and easier for the dog to hear. You can also stretch out the word 'yee-haa', which. terminates in another open vowel. 'Come', on the other hand, has a very blunt, aggressive effect and terminates with a conso-nant, which is not very good for calling this command with sufficient volume from far away. Try a test: position yourself and your partner 50 metres apart. Now call your partner the way you would call your dog, and vice versa. You will be amazed how little comes back to you. Dogs' hearing is similar to humans' – only the higher and lower frequency range is a little more extended.

Learning cues

You have decided on a word or a whistle; now you need to explain the meaning of this cue to your dog.

Put your dog on the lead; a five-metre line is enough to start off with. Take particularly good treats with you and go to an open space without distractions.

Move away from your dog after your command. He is obliged to follow you!

Now call your dog by his name and say 'Here' or whistle afterwards. Please do it only once! The 'here' should be called in the same way that you intend to use later. Otherwise it is difficult for your dog to understand at first that an abrupt 'here' means the same thing as 'heeee-yer'. Choose one variant and stick with it.

Straight after you have given your command, move backwards away from the dog. This will make your dog want to follow you.

Once your dog has caught up with you, affirm his action straight away with a treat.

Dogs are programmed for movement; they perceive movement considerably more effectively than they do stationary objects. This is why you should not stand as if rooted to the spot when recalling your dog. It is not usually a case of disobedience when your dog races past you; he is simply not seeing you or taking you in. Make it easy for your dog to come to you: when calling, always move away from him a little bit so that he is obliged to follow you. This way, you kill two birds with one stone: you make yourself easily recognisable for your dog (movement), and you trigger a certain group dynamic in him: he wants to follow you.

Dogs do it the same way with each other. Just watch dogs chasing: they see each other from a distance and, once eye contact has been made, the initiator of the game races off and the other dog follows him.

Please do not ask for a 'sit'! Your dog is meant to be rewarded for coming to you, not for a 'sit'. Your dog needs to internalise one thing: that he is rewarded immediately when he comes. Important! 'Here' always means 'here', directly in front of your feet. There is no 'sort of here' or 'halfway here'.

Your dog is with you – he gets his reward for this immediately.

If it is preferable to affirm your dog's actions using toys, note the following: once your dog has caught up with you, pull the toy out of your pocket immediately and play with your dog straight away. However, do not throw the toy!

If your dog does not give the toy back on command, you should hold off using this variant of reinforcement until your dog has learned to give the toy back without being urged to do so. In this case, it is advisable to use treats that your dog really likes. The chapter 'Rewards – your dog's wages' tells you how to identify these treats.

After affirmation, send him off again with a jolly 'Off you go!'

Once your dog has gained a good grasp of the command for coming back in areas without distractions, you can start increasing the surrounding stimuli. He needs to come well and truly haring up to you when you call him. Depending on the breed, even an immediately initiated detour in your direction is enough. After all, herding dogs are not as zippy as some border collies. The important thing is to introduce the dog to the various distractions gradually and not to demand the impossible from him straight away. Remember that dogs learn in specific contexts! It will be a while, when there are bigger distractions around, until he performs something that he did beautifully when there were no distractions. If you raise the requirement too

Send your dog off again with a command. He is now allowed to do what he likes again.

soon, your frustration will increase, your dog will stop enjoying coming up to you and it will be the same old story once again. Your dog will have no desire to come if he has to decide whether you are in a good mood or annoyed again. You must never present your dog with this dilemma – he has to know that things are always good with you.

Extending waiting time

If you call your dog to you, there's a certain reason for it. You want him to come to you because you are going to put him on the lead or because people or cyclists are coming and he needs to wait. This is why it is important to stop giving the treats straight away. Once you have mastered the first training phase (see previous chapter) and your dog has understood the cue, you need to start with two things: firstly, gradually discontinuing the treats for coming; and secondly, making the dog sit after coming.

At the same time, it is important that your dog performs a reliable 'sit' at the first attempt. If you are still having no success with the 'sit' or, as before with your old 'come' command, you have been inconsistent, you need to build it up again using a new word (see chapter 'Building up a command, using the 'sit' as an example).

Call your dog, move away from him and praise him verbally. once he has caught up with you. Your dog is actually expecting the treat now.

He will look at you expectantly. While he is doing so, say 'Sit' and in return he will get the reward immediately he has his bottom on the ground. Ensure that the reward is given while the dog is in the 'sit' position. You want to reward your dog for sitting down, not for standing up!

What the dog is actually expecting from you now is the treat, but he needs to learn how to wait.

Now let your dog sit. Now affirm his action in the 'sit' position with a treat.

Send your dog straight off again with an 'Off you go!' If, however, your dog continues to jump about around you, simply ignore him. After all, he is free to focus his attention on his own business now.

LIMERICK COUNTY LIBRARY

Summary: recall training structure

- 1. Learning cues
  Start gently.
- Call your dog using your new cue ('Fido – here') or using the whistle.
- Call/whistle only once!
- Move backwards away from your dog.
- Affirm your dog's action immediately he has caught up with you.
- Send him straight off again with an 'Off you go!' and a dismissing hand movement.
- 2. Consolidating cue
  Increase the surrounding stimuli.
- Open space with cyclist and pedestrian path nearby.
- In the woods.
- In the park.
- 3. Extending waiting time next to the dog trainer.
- Only affirm your dog's action once you have got him to sit.
- Pay attention to eye contact – see 'Name game' exercise in the chapter 'Accompanying training'.
- Send him away again after a few seconds with 'Off you go!'.
- 4. Consolidating coming and waiting.
- Affirm a different way each time. Over the next two weeks, only give a treat for every other time the dog comes and sits.
- After that, for the next two weeks, only give a reward every third time the dog comes and sits, and so on. Vary the treat, as well: something especially good one time, then something average. Remember that you have written down your dog's choice in your rewards list. Even champagne and caviar every day can get boring after a while.

Important!

Do not call your dog every time there's something interesting going on along the way. This may get him paying more attention to his surroundings and encourage him to shoot off at the worst possible moment.

Do not do the recall training more frequently than three to four times in one walk. Go for a walk together every day. Take part in your dog's world, too. If your dog stops and sniffs about interestedly, go up to him and take a look at what's so interesting. It's the same thing with dogs as well. If one dog has found a promising mouse-hole, the other dogs will follow, so give it a try the other way around: stop and look totally fascinated by a tree or a bush; when your dog notices, he will come and have a look at the great thing you're gazing at.

Slow down or stop – maintaining the radius

Tie a knot in the line about 1.5 metres away from the end. This knot is your signal that you now need to tell your dog to go more slowly. This is actually one of the easier exercises that become engrained on a walk. The more often you do it, the sooner your dog will understand what you expect from him.

You feel the knot in your hand and say to your dog: 'Fido – slooowly', then you stand still for a moment. (There must be a consequence to every command: in this case, standing still.)

Your dog should now also stop, with a glance back at you. Praise immediately.

In this case the use of a clicker would be the most accurate way to let the dog know what he's done correctly.

Send him off again with an 'Off you go!' immediately after the praise.

This way you incidentally teach him another important command – slowing down.

By way of variation, if you want your dog to stop on 'Stop', then instead of 'Slooowly' say 'Stop' and stand still. You should practise this on a normal two-metre line at first.

Important! There is no pulling on the 10-metre line – there is strictly no pulling on any line. If your dog pulls on the 10-metre line, you should intensify the orientation training! The 10-metre line needs to be a matter of course for your dog.

As soon as your dog starts making his way towards you, praise him lavishly (or click and reward).

You must stand still after the command 'Stop'.

Learning cues

You run with your dog on the two-metre line, say 'Stop' and stand still.

Your dog should now also stand still.

Go to your dog and give him the treat in this standing position. Your dog needs to learn to stand still after a stop and wait until you are next to him or until you give the command later. Cancel the exercise with a 'Go on.'

Once the stop exercise is working on the two-metre line (stop – go up – treat – continue), take the five-metre line and practise the same at a greater distance. Once this is a success as well, you can use the 10-metre line for training.

The important thing is that your dog learns to wait until further instructions from you or until you come to him. As long as your dog neither comes reliably nor pays much attention to you when running free, the long line remains attached to your dog at all times. Do not allow your dog to make mistakes. This applies to puppies and older dogs alike. This way, you always have your dog under control and can intervene at the right time, especially at the beginning.

Your dog stands still on 'Stop', so you can now go up to him. Reward your dog in this position, too.

Structured training

In many cases, dogs have no problem coming back on the long line when there are no big distractions. However, as soon as there is another dog around, it is a different story. At our dog school, we are lucky to have a lot of outdoor space and a kind farmer who doesn't grumble, even we train on his freshly mown fields. The more often you practise coming back on a line in the group, the easier it is to call your dog back from playing later on, even without the line.

Long-line training in a group – open field

How are we going to get it to work without getting all entangled in the lines? It's very simple. Firstly, you need a lot of space. Secondly, you need enough routine in dealing with the long line. Then the training is no problem. Three of you can easily go and practise on a freshly mown crop field. In principle, the sequence is quite easy: you stand with your dog on the long line so far apart from each other that the dogs can meet effortlessly in the middle.

The long line is almost entirely used up in the process. Once the dogs have met in the middle, let them sniff each other a bit and play – make sure that there are no entanglements – then call your dogs off. At first you'll have to help out a little bit – please make sure, particularly with a smaller dog, that you don't turn this into a flying lesson. Draw your dog back gently. Remember to distance yourself from the dogs when you call them. Cheer your dog when he manages to separate himself from the other dogs and comes running up to you. Even if you had to help and reminded him that you have 'the power', praise him lavishly when he's next to you. Then send your dog straight off again. After all, he's keen to be back with the other dogs.

As a variant, you can also train in a group where only your dog is on the long line. Here, though, the other dogs need to be so advanced in their training that they are able to be called out of a playing group without any problems.

When training in a group, you should always stand far enough apart from each other to prevent major lead entanglements.

Otherwise, it will be extremely counterproductive, as your dog will then be constantly mobbed by dogs that cannot be called back. Additionally, you should make sure that the dogs do not get tangled up in the line. Until you've had some practice with the long line, you should avoid this exercise.

Chair circle

Form a circle of chairs with a diameter of about five to six metres. All dogs are on a five-metre long line and next to their humans, who are sitting on chairs. Now, just one single dog is let loose. He is allowed to move about freely and is called back again after approximately five seconds. There's a great treat for him as soon as he's back with you. At first, you'll still be reeling in your dog, but after a few rounds your dog will understand what it's about: coming back.

Always do the sending off and calling back in turns. While one dog is permitted to move about, this is additionally an exercise in impulse control for the other dogs. Make sure that the unemployed dogs keep themselves occupied with their humans. As the rounds progress, reduce the circle of chairs to a diameter of approximately three metres and play this game again. It is important that your dog learns that the fun is not over when he is called out of a group of dogs.

Waiting and coming back is practised in the circle of chairs.

When conducting long-line training with aggression problems, it is important to start from far away, where the dog does not yet react and is completely relaxed.

Long-line training with aggression problems

Aggression towards humans and fellow dogs is probably the most difficult issue and, in most cases, needs to be taken very seriously. If you are aware that your dog reacts overly aggressively, you should do something about it.

Many people only walk their dogs at times when they will not meet anyone else. You can make much better use of this time by completing training where the emphasis is on obedience and attentiveness.

In this chapter, I explain the method for desensitisation and counterconditioning, which involves small training steps towards replacing the unpleasant sensations that your dog expresses through aggression with – ideally – pleasant sensations. With dogs that have aggression problems, it is absolutely essential that they are able to turn round on command, that they are highly responsive and that they enjoy following the signals from their human. For you, this means dealing with your dog in a friendly and self-controlled manner at all times, particularly where there are aggression problems.

Transforming feelings

The training described in the orientation training section is particularly fundamental for dogs with aggression problems. It is essential that you conduct this training. The second exercise that you should practise is the name game from the 'Accompanying training' chapter. It needs to be 100 per cent clear to your dog that his name means something particularly good. Discipline yourself: do not talk to your dog the whole day long. Deal out your words sparingly. When you say something to your dog, it

This snarl is clear: the dog is warning off his opponent. (Photo: Gutmann)

needs to be something important. Otherwise you will be demoting yourself to background noise. When you talk meaninglessly to your dog all day, how is he meant to know that there is a serious relevance for him when you say important things like 'look' or 'sit'? You're sure to know situations where you talk to your dog with things like: 'Fido, it's great here isn't it?' or: 'Haven't we got lovely weather at the moment, eh, Fido?'. Your dog does not understand you. He understands only that his meaningless name has cropped up again and nothing is happening. How is he meant to tell the difference between the inconsequential phrases above and an important 'Sit, Fido'? If, to cap it all, you start screaming at your barking dog caught up in the lead: 'Fido, get out!' and 'Aaargh! Fido!', you are declaring to your dog that you are just as agitated as he is, and this way you only reinforce the behaviour. Oddly, people often do this for years without seeing any change in the conduct (unwanted barking on the lead).

Remember: dogs learn by association! What association is your dog going to make, therefore, if you scream at him or – even worse – punish him for barking on the lead or growling when encountering other dogs? Either that his human is just as agitated as he is, or that the unknown dog is bad. If you do that often enough, you are declaring to your dog that all unknown dogs are bad. In the worst case, you are bringing up a dog that will knock down all oncoming quadrupeds immediately and without warning when off the lead. After all, he hasn't learned any better. Additionally, he continually receives the feedback that this strategy works for him, as he is commonly the victor in

these clashes. The verdict is then pronounced: the dog is dominant and deserves to brought up particularly severely. Please ponder in your heart of hearts whether you as the owner do not secretly think it's great to call such a dominant dog your own. There is often a reason why your dog keeps picking fights: because you let him. Change your attitude! It is not very pleasant for anyone around you to encounter dogs like these.

A dog that is constantly subjected to loutish behaviour is likely to react with similar aggression, except out of different motives. A possible name for a dog like this is a 'nervous biter' that has simply developed a strategy: attack is the best defence. Dogs like these immediately associate unpleasant sensations and fear with the sight of a dog or anything resembling a dog. The dog tries to get away, but is for the most part unable to. This is why he starts bounding about on the lead – the dog wants the source of the fear to disappear fast – or, if the dog is off the lead, there is likewise immediate baring of teeth and bullying. The result: most dogs stay well away. The nervous dog has also achieved what he needed: distance from the other dogs at the source of the fear. In many cases, these dogs that go on the offensive out of fear are also considered dominant. Please note the following phrase: dogs do what they do. They cannot change their spots. They do not understand us when we talk to them. This is why it falls to us humans to help our dogs out of these tricky situations. Dogs would be able to keep out of one another's way on an open hunting ground, but in our towns and villages, where leads are often mandatory, this is unfortunately not necessarily the case.

With long-line training, slowly and with each dog's requirements in mind, we first of all attempt to restore a little freedom to these awkward customers. Most dogs with these types of problems only go out of doors on a two-metre line. Secondly, we need to eliminate our dog's unpleasant sensations with regard to unknown dogs and gradually replace them with pleasant sensations. In most cases, this works successfully through food. Eating is a primary need of every single living being. Eating brings contentment!

Summary:
starting the desensitisation
  + Do the orientation training.
  + Play the name game described
    in the chapter 'Accompanying training'.
    The name can only be something
    positive for your dog.
  + Reconstruct the 'sit' exercise with
    the emphasis on the positive!
    Choose a new word for it: this can
    even be Greek or Italian. Your dog
    must only have positive associations
    with sitting on command and perform
    it reliably in all places.
    See the chapter: 'Building up a
    command, using the 'sit' as an example'.

Orientation training for aggressive dogs

The training for an 'average dog', complete with training schedule, is described in the section, 'Orientation training' for all age categories. The training for aggressive dogs is based on this. To start off with, ensure that you seek out an open space with no distraction at all (no cycle path nearby, open country). You have your dog, the 10-metre line and plenty of really good treats. It all hangs on your dog's motivation! You will find the procedure for the orientation training in the chapter, 'Preparatory training'.

To start off with, always train at locations where there is no distraction for the dog. The distraction is increased continuously during the course of the training. Proceed nice and slowly.

Our intention with the following training schedule is to make the aggressive dog responsive and convince him that unknown humans or dogs are not as bad as all that. We want your dog to learn to associate good things with other dogs/humans and to seek out contact with them.

Levels of distraction – duration of training

1. Open space without distraction – approximately two to three weeks' orientation training as above.

You will most often find open land with no distractions outside your town or village or in isolated corners of parks. If you train in inner-city parks, please ensure that you're less likely to encounter dogs off the lead. In big cities

With another dog around, practise things that your dog can already do and reward him for this again and again.
This terrier is willing to concentrate and take no notice of the other dog for a piece of cheese.

there's always a little piece of open land somewhere that's not busy. When heading off to open land outside, don't forget your poop bag and make sure that the grass is short – you should avoid entering fields where the grass is more than ankle-deep. These are fields for food crops, and farmers do not always react in a friendly manner when an owner runs across these fields with his or her dog. Seek out three to four different training locations.

2. Open space with unknown person or dog – orientation training.

Make arrangements with a friend who is going to assist you. Discuss the things that you want to train with your friend beforehand:

- Location of the training. You need to park in different spots – out of sight.
- What do you want your assistant to do? Write a to-do list.
- How long do you intend to train?

Alternatively, communication by means of mobile phone is always a very good opportunity for a little spontaneity. Under no circumstances should you attempt to yell instructions across a 100-metre distance. This is no help at all and will only make your dog nervous.

Drive off to a quiet open space with your dog. Let your dog get out and take a quiet sniff around to explore the surroundings first. Your dog is, of course, on the long line throughout. Your assistant has parked at another end of the open space and is far away enough from you (with or without dog, depending on what your dog reacts aggressively to) to prevent your dog from jumping on the person/dog. Start with two to three rounds of the orientation training and then practise a few exercises such as 'sit' and 'lie down'. If your dog reacts to people, your assistant should keep moving about on the field the whole time, but always at the agreed distance.

If your dog has a problem with other dogs, letting the assistant stand still with his or her dog is enough. Of course, the assistant's dog should not react aggressively to other dogs himself.

You should not perform the training units (orientation training and a few exercises) for longer than 10 minutes at the very most. Your dog must not react. If you notice your dog getting anxious and looking across at the assistant all the time, play with him a bit and then put him in the car. It is enormously important to always put your dog in the car when he is calm. Even if you've only been training for five minutes, it doesn't matter! The main thing is that your dog gets into the car calmly. If you believe that your dog has learned nothing this way, think again! He has learned to be calm in the presence of a human/dog and not to be aggressive – learning is a continuous process. Simply have another dog lie down when you start the joint training. Your dog will notice the unknown dog – remember that dogs' perception is significantly different and more refined. He only needs to catch this other dog's scent, or maybe see his outline through the grass – which is fine, as long as your dog is calm and relaxed at the same time. If your dog is aggressive towards people, you should start with just a person at this stage.

During the brief training units, practise things that your dog can already do or fine-tune new exercises. The only important thing is that you do something with your dog in the presence of the trigger and always reward this activity. Don't forget to pack particularly good treats: eating brings contentment.

You should repeat this exercise two to three times daily, but please allow a break of at least one hour between the training units. Do not go for a walk, play ball or similar. Your dog is meant to rest. Do not forget to write down immediately what you have been training, with whom, where and for how long. Make a list of unusual incidents, and how your dog and you reacted.

Potential problems and solutions

Is your dog leaping away, barking, getting caught in the lead and trying to get to the person/dog?

Remain calm and still, and do not talk to the dog. You are the rock in stormy seas and must simply wait until your dog has calmed down again and turns round to face you. As a rapid-fire solution, you can also increase the distance, although that is not exactly what we wanted because it tells your dog that he can get away from you by barking. You should note the distance in your training diary for next time. Once your dog is calm, call him in a friendly voice. Now have him do approximately three exercises one after another, for example 'sit', 'lie down' and 'paw'. Reward him for the 'paw'. It is important that after an aggressive incident you have your dog do something else, so that the time interval between aggression and reward is long enough. Otherwise, you might unintentionally build yourself an unpleasant sequence of behaviour: bark at dog + look at human = reward. In this case, we would have achieved precisely the opposite of what we actually want to do.

Should this overreaction occur, then you were too close to the trigger or something else happened; were you perhaps annoyed, stressed or a little bit anxious at that particular moment? Check your records and start the next training session again with a bigger distance and in a better mood.

Increasing distraction/ reducing distance

Start raising the requirements slowly. However, remember when doing so that you should only ever change one requirement: when training on new terrain, maintain a bigger distance between you and your assistant/dog. Your dog has enough to do with taking in the new environment and working with you. When you raise one requirement you must always make something else easier, so you should never start any new exercises on unfamiliar terrain. Do things that your dog can do really well. The main thing is to keep your dog busy. Practise things with the clicker: nudging your hand with his nose, looking, raising a paw or have your dog hunt for treats.

Let your assistant get a little closer during the subsequent training units. Remember to concentrate on your dog! Do not wait on tenterhooks for a reaction from your dog – if you do, it will happen. Continue to work with your dog and reward him for good behaviour, well-performed exercises and willingness to co-operate. However, do not proceed too quickly. Keep an eye on your dog, and if you notice him getting anxious do a few familiar and basic exercises and finish the training. Seek out three to four training locations, where you train with your assistant (preferably alternating assistants) on a continual basis. With a problem like this, desensitising a dog can take several months. After all, this problem did not pop up over night – it had months and in most cases even years to take hold. Do not start the next section until you are able to pass the standing person/other dog calmly at a distance of approximately five metres.

Walking in parallel

So far, you have only been doing exercises standing still. It is time to get a move on. Ask a second assistant to train with you – preferably a family member or good friend whom your dog really likes. Head off to a training location that your dog particularly enjoys and where there is as little distraction as possible. Your first assistant positions himself or herself alongside you, at a distance where your dog does not yet react.

Your second assistant positions himself or herself in the middle as a kind of barrier in between. Remember to shorten the lead according to how close to each other you are, so that your dog cannot get to the unknown person or dog if he does react.

Start walking together, remaining parallel at all times and keeping the friendly person in the middle. Start with the same distance between you as during your very first training unit. Please always move really slowly as you do so.

Maintain enough distance away from the trigger and work with your dog in a calm and concentrated manner. The second assistant walks in the middle, acting as a partition.

Why? The faster you walk, the more agitated and hectic the training situation becomes, and your dog will soon become tempted to react. If your dog looks at you, you should affirm his action immediately (treat). The most precise way is by means of the clicker. The clicker has the added benefit that the click triggers pleasant sensations and joyful expectation in the dog in any case (see the chapter, 'Clicker training').

Once you have been up and down this way a few times, finish the training unit and take a break for at least one hour. Train this parallel walking on your other practice grounds, gradually reducing the distance as you go along.

As the next variant, once your dog is able to walk at an acceptable distance (approximately three to five metres) alongside a person/dog, at all training locations, then add a second person/dog. Here, again, start with your dog's favourite location and keep a sufficient distance: that is, the distance that you kept right at the start of your training. You can normally make

Neither dog is interested in the other. The assistant in the middle acts as an optical 'partition.

Distract your dog with a hunt for treats as your assistant passes by.

the transition to reducing the distance again pretty quickly, but always remember to finish the training unit promptly while your dog is still able to deal with the situation calmly. Practise it again at your usual training locations, as well. Perhaps you will find even more friendly assistants and dog-owners with self-controlled dogs that can help you with your problem. Set yourself a goal along the way: for example, your dog is required to walk calmly with 10 people alongside at a distance of five metres. This way, you will have something to work towards. Once this goal has been achieved, treat yourself and your dog to a glass of champers and a lovely bone – the latter being for your lovely dog, of course! In real life, though, people do not always walk in parallel to one another. This is why you should also train the following. As always, start in your dog's favourite open space, with an assistant. The assistant stands opposite you at the distance that was required at the start of the training. Now move towards each other within this distance. Make sure that the line is short enough to prevent your dog from reaching the person. Continue walking casually and calmly as your assistant comes towards you. Affirm your dog's action every time he makes eye contact (clicker). You must not stint on the treats! Eating brings contentment and provides a distraction. If you are working without a clicker, it is a good idea to play a quick treat-hunting game with your dog as your assistant passes by.

Your dog is still aware of the person/dog, but is too occupied to be bothered about him. Here, again, start switching locations and reducing the distance. Only start continually raising the requirements once your dog is really laid-back when you train with your assistant. Raising the

requirements too quickly is counterproductive and only generates frustration in you, which in turn is transmitted to the dog. It can therefore be a number of weeks and months until you have achieved the outcome that you set your sights on.

People do not always creep along like snails, so you need to start quickening the pace – at least, your assistant does. The assistant starts with a gentle trot, jogging, running fast, running and yelling. Reward all forms of calm behaviour! You can also work with a food tube

You can distract the dog continuously using the food tube. Your dog is aware of the other one, but associates the positive experience of the food with the unknown dog.

Dogs enjoy licking a well-filled food tube.

your dog encounters others. A food tube contains delicious things like liver sausage, pâté and similar, and can be refilled and rinsed out. The procedure is that the jogger comes towards you whilst the dog licks the food tube.

Once your dog has stopped reacting to one jogger, you can start increasing the number of people again. If your dog stays cool, the joggers start coming from different directions. Take care at all times to reward your dog for all forms of feedback and calm behaviour, and to stop the training at the right moment. This is the number one rule for this training method!

Approaching head–on

We need to tackle this as well at some point. If you have come this far, with all training steps and distractions – congratulations! Please keep constant checks on anything that hasn't gone the way you'd planned it. Again, ask an assistant to approach you head-on. Start at a place where your dog does not react. If the dog sees the assistant and looks at you afterwards: click and reward, make it clear that you're delighted and throw a treat for your dog. Walk up to the approaching person slowly in a semi-circle, say